THE
**Irresistible
Church** SERIES

D1615659

Start with HELLO

Start with
HELLO

Introducing Your Church to
SPECIAL NEEDS MINISTRY

by Kate Brueck

 THE **IRRESISTIBLE CHURCH** SERIES

Copyright © 2015 Joni and Friends

Start with Hello
ISBN 978-0-9965522-0-2

Written by Kate Brueck
Contributors: Debbie Lillo and Stacy Hodge
Contributing Editors: Ali Howard and Mike Dobes
Editor-in-Chief: Marc Stein

All rights reserved. No part of this book may be used or reproduced in any
manner whatsoever without the written permission of the publisher.

Printed in the United States of America.

Scripture quotations are taken from the Holy Bible, English Standard Version®,
copyright © 2001 by Crossway Bibles, a publishing ministry of Good News
Publishers. Used by permission. All rights reserved.

Produced by The Denzel Agency (www.denzel.org)
Cover and Interior Design: Rob Williams

For information or to order additional print copies of this
and other resources contact:

Joni and Friends International Disability Center
P.O. Box 3333, Agoura Hills, California 91376-3333
Email: churchrelations@joniandfriends.org
Phone: 818-707-5664

Kindle version available at www.irresistiblechurch.org

CONTENTS

Before You Begin 9

Five Steps to Launching a Special Needs Ministry 13

Step 1: **Ask**.. 15
Step 2: **Listen** 29
Step 3: **Plan** 33
Step 4: **Train** 53
Step 5: **Launch** 63

The Blessings 67
The *Irresistible* Church 69

Before You Begin

"I've read books on disability ministry, but what do I do first? Where do I go from here?" So starts a conversation we have had with multiple volunteers, parents, and ministry leaders across the country. These people love God, love their churches, and love individuals affected by special needs. However, they have been stuck between believing the reasons why we should embark on this journey and knowing how to actually begin.

This may be the first resource you have read regarding launching a special needs ministry. If so, you should know that there are many other valuable books on disability ministry available as well. We can recommend several to you that have been helpful to thousands along this journey. 🕮 You may have already worked through several of those resources. Whether this is the first or the hundredth one you have picked up, we pray this small booklet will give you direction and help you implement a fruitful ministry.

🕮 This symbol indicates that there are supplemental resources that correspond with this topic at http://www.joniandfriends.org/church-relations/

Words Have Meaning

Aiming for "fruitful ministry" sounds biblical and holy, but what does that actually mean? According to *Merriam-Webster Online* (2015), the term *ministry* can mean "a person or thing through which something is accomplished."[1] We often equate ministry with programs in the church, but it is really just the means by which something gets done, the avenue by which a goal is accomplished. So, from the very beginning of your journey with special needs ministry, we encourage you to release the idea that disability ministry equals another church program. This ministry may involve several existing church programs, it may be its own program, or it may never have an official program "home," but that does not determine its fruitfulness.

The "fruitfulness" portion of ministry is a biblical term—one that demonstrates an individual has been raised to new life in Jesus Christ. Fruitfulness starts with "new birth" in a person by grace through faith in the saving person and work of Jesus (John 3:3, Ephesians 2:8). It is demonstrated when people who were once dead in their sins exhibit God's love, joy, peace, patience, kindness, goodness, faithfulness, gentleness, and self-control through the amazing, sanctifying work of the Holy Spirit (Galatians 5:22–23, Colossians 3:12).

Ultimately, the goal of fruitful special needs ministry is eternal: that all people would know the good news of Jesus Christ and that disciples would be made (Matthew 28:19). In doing so, the body of Christ, the church, would be made complete (Luke 14:23) while exhibiting the character of Jesus who is the Head (Colossians 1:18). Referring back to our definition of "fruitful," whatever person or thing God uses to accomplish this in the lives of special needs families exemplifies a fruitful special needs ministry.

Irresistible Church

Instead of creating another program, let us examine what the church would look like if everyone, regardless of special needs or extraordinary abilities, were embraced as a fully functioning member of Christ's body. Regardless of cognitive processing, verbal communication, behavioral struggles, or physical ability, each member would be valued as a person flawlessly created in the image of God, and the church family would receive each member's God-given gifts with joy.

Such a church would be irresistible, not just to the special needs family looking to be loved for who they are, but for anyone skeptical that the church holds a place for them. The unemployed, the addict, the chronically ill, the divorced, the widow, the young single, the orphan, the perfectionist, the insecure, the average Joe or Jane—each would recognize the unconditional love of such a church by seeing how those with disabilities belong unconditionally.

This larger dream requires change. The change needed is easy to name but takes effort to implement.

When we ask people with disabilities what they desire in a church, they overwhelmingly share two dreams: accessibility and acceptance. Accessibility to existing structures, programs, and people is imperative. Acceptance with a sense of belonging extended from others who also use and benefit from the structures, programs, and fellowship of the church is equally necessary.

Accessibility and acceptance usually grow when a group of people understands God's attitude toward those with disabilities. This group then uses the church's strengths and mission to develop a solid plan. So, how do you step into starting this "solid plan"?

Notes
1. Merriam-Webster Online, s.v. "ministry," accessed June 26, 2015, http://www.merriam-webster.com/dictionary/ministry.

Five Steps to Launching a Special Needs Ministry

I f we drew a road map with the following five steps on it and gave it to everyone wanting to start a special needs ministry, we would see as many different routes as there are people. Most churches take at least a year to complete the journey, while some churches have taken over a decade to become a fully inclusive church. No special needs ministry is going to look exactly like another—nor should it. We are addressing the needs and gifts of people, all unique and strategically placed by God in his body, so we should expect God to uniquely and creatively orchestrate ways to make his body accessible and accepting.

The steps are simple: ask, listen, plan, train, and launch. Please do not think these five steps are a magical formula for a thriving special needs ministry, but recognize these five steps can help you organize your church's response to a very real need. We pray that this organized action plan will provide direction, clarity, and a way for you to share God's purpose with the rest of your church.

Step 1: Ask

Ask God

You can have a brilliant plan developed and agreed upon by brilliant, hardworking people and it can fail. The key ingredient we have found missing in that scenario is the Holy Spirit. As Psalm 127:1 says, "Unless the LORD builds the house, those who build it labor in vain." This is God's church, God's mission, God's eternal purpose, and God's people, so we can and should expect God to be central in disability ministry.

Before you ask anyone else, ask God. Seek him in prayer. Read his Word. Ask God to prepare the hearts of leadership, the congregation, and families with special needs. Ask God to send workers into this specific field of harvest—where workers are very few. Ask God for wisdom as you proceed down this path (James 1:5). Be patient and wait on the Lord for each step.

This step of asking God is never finished. It is the first step and a continual action in every other step that follows (1 Thessalonians 5:17). Including the leadership and other members of your church body in asking God what ministry he has for your church helps foster a deep sense of unity and community.

Ask Your Leadership

Asking God to accomplish this work is imperative. Asking for your leadership's blessing and support is also necessary. Without the process of asking, you will have several groups of highly invested people (including yourself!) who have varying expectations and fears.

Your church's head leadership probably carefully crafted a church mission statement. This statement guides everything your leadership pursues, allows, and supports.

Your church's mission statement acts as the trajectory for all that happens within the church—including disability ministry. Imagine you are shooting a bow and arrow at a target across a field. You aim in a specific direction at a specific height to allow the arrow to gracefully arc to the bull's-eye. The mission statement is the formula for hitting that bull's-eye. You might have discovered that the current programs, mindsets, and environments do not launch families or individuals with special needs all the way to the target, but that does not mean the mission statement is wrong. We might have to change the bow, or shoot into the wind, or walk closer to the target, or use a host of other supports to get the arrow all the way to the bull's-eye, but you certainly cannot aim in another direction and expect spectacular results.

Sometimes starting a special needs ministry feels like accomplishing a new and different mission because you are seeking a change in how things are currently done. However, the good news in all of this is that your church's mission statement already includes people with special needs and their families, whether it was written with that intention or not. For example, one church lives by the statement, "Inviting all people into a loving relationship with Jesus Christ." Because "all people" includes people with disabilities, this church pursued a formal special needs ministry and now fully includes several families with special needs.

Your church is already on a mission and hopes that you, as a church member, are on that mission too. Therefore, take a good, long look at your existing mission statement before you meet with your pastor or leadership team. Ask: How do all people, all with different needs and abilities, already fit into our mission? What is our church currently pursuing? Approaching your church leadership with these topics can open up a very productive and positive conversation.

In addition, ask for your leadership's blessing and support as you survey your congregation and community for the specific needs and desires of families affected by disability. Find out which church leader will ultimately be responsible for special needs ministry endeavors. As you move through this journey, keep your leadership partner informed, celebrate God's provision together, and support them as they interact with other leaders and members of the congregation.

Ask the People you Aim to Serve

Michelle's Story

Michelle and I sat down on a park bench on a blustery fall day, coffee in hand. I probed her heart and mind, asking what life is like for her and her husband to raise a son with autism and a younger daughter in our church. I wanted to know the good, the bad, and the ugly. What hurts had been sustained through the years? Why did they choose our church? What blessings had they experienced? What service and community had they enjoyed? We discussed her dreams for her children, how she desires them to grow in grace, serve in the kingdom, and be totally included in the body.

Michelle graciously answered my queries until, suddenly surprised, she said, "This is the first time I've shared some of these thoughts with anyone. No one has asked me these questions, or taken the time to work through the answers."

A few months later, Michelle shared with me that our conversation started a healing process in her heart. Michelle now works on staff in the children's ministry and has pulled a team of people together to form an effective special needs ministry.

I share Michelle's story because while simply asking is something that seems so small, so commonplace, it is actually the best place to start.

The Reason We Ask

How do you find out what would allow families to plug in at your church? How do you know what environment would be best for that eight-year-old girl with Down syndrome, or that fourteen-year-old boy with autism, or that middle-aged man who is nonverbal? How do you know if they know Jesus? How do you know what programs would be helpful or in what ministries the family is longing to take part? You ask.

This type of conversation takes time and effort and may involve a home visit. It could mean bringing along another like-minded soul to attend the person with special needs so the caregiver can complete his or her thoughts and sentences. It certainly means a face-to-face, earnest, open conversation about a family and their needs.

While having this type of conversation with Michelle, she verbalized how grateful her family was for the supports put into place to include their young son with autism, but she shared how she worried that he was not actually learning about Jesus. Her main hindrance to bringing up her concerns was the fear that the leadership and volunteers who developed the plan might think her ungrateful and whiny. By bringing Michelle into the conversation and allowing her desires, dreams, and insider knowledge to shape the ministry plan, a young boy with autism is receiving the benefits of discipleship.

First Things First

We hope, like many ministry leaders we have talked with, you are now exclaiming, "But that's just common sense!" Exactly! And yet we often receive puzzled questions from eager volunteers who dream of providing a special needs ministry but of which no one takes advantage. These kindhearted folks walk away from ministry wondering what went wrong.

When asked if they talked with the people they aimed to serve first, the answer is almost always no.

Ministry leaders who take extra time and effort to meet one-on-one with each family or individual affected by special needs always learn valuable information that shapes future ministry efforts. Skipping this step is like trying to decorate a house in the dark: walls may get painted, pictures may get hung, and furniture may be placed, but when daylight comes, no one will want to live there.

Your church may already have an intake form to help place students with special needs into your children's or youth programs, and that can be very helpful. It does not, however, replace this heart-to-heart, comprehensive conversation. We call this initial conversation the Family Ministry Profile.

Family Ministry Profile

The following interview outline is based on that first conversation with Michelle. It has proven helpful time after time with new families and new ministry endeavors. It is not a magic formula, but it can be a good starting place for gaining a comprehensive understanding of a family you want to support and include. Pray together and let the Holy Spirit guide your conversation.

Family Church Involvement

- How long have you attended our church?
- What brought you here?
- How is our church already meeting the unique needs of your family?
- What has hurt your family in the past regarding your family's special needs?
- What parts of church life do you and your family desire to participate in?
- What prevents your family from participating in and serving in church programs?
- What supports are necessary for you and your family to fully participate in the body of Christ?
- What are your immediate needs, inside or outside the church?

Disability Profile

- Name of child with a disability:
- Gender:
- Age and school placement:
- Participates in (church ministries):
- Disability:
- This disability manifests itself in the following ways:

- This child loves the following:
- What do you need us to know or understand about this child?
- Does this child have any triggers?
- Are there any activities that can calm this child if he or she is feeling overwhelmed?

Child Discipleship Profile

- The child with a disability would best be discipled (choose the appropriate answers):
  - In the typical setting for the child's age group with no supports
  - In the typical setting for the child's age group with a buddy who is:
    - An adult
    - An older student
    - A peer
  - In a separate classroom with a trained teacher and other students with special needs
  - A combination of the above choices that would look like_____

  _____

  _____

  _____

  _____

- Why do you believe your child will grow spiritually in this setting?
- Why do you believe your child will not grow spiritually in other settings?
- What is your child's current spiritual state?
- What is your dream for your child spiritually?

Sibling(s) Discipleship Profile

- Name of sibling:
- Gender:
- Age and school placement:
- Participates in (church ministries):
- This child is affected by his or her sibling's disability in the following ways:
- What is your child's current spiritual state?
- What do you believe would benefit your child spiritually?
- What is your dream for your child spiritually?

Follow-Up

- Who else would benefit from this conversation?

Moving Forward

You will notice that these questions are quite open-ended, and they will hopefully lead to pertinent questions of your own. They also purposefully focus on spiritual growth, not social skills, motor-skills, therapies, or academic objectives. While those considerations may play a role in how a person is ultimately included, our purpose in asking is to focus on the eternal goal. Parents are constantly advocating for their kids in the world of education, enrichment activities, and medicine. Although the church can be helpful in all areas, the church is not ultimately an extension of these services and should not be expected to fulfill those functions. Instead, from the very beginning, allow the church to be the church: a place for worship, community, service, and growth.

You will also notice that the entire family is taken into consideration—not just the person with the disability. Siblings are often intensely affected by their brother's or sister's special needs and can feel ignored, abandoned, jealous, overprotective, and like a responsible caregiver by turns. Many siblings become their brother's or sister's default buddy and caregiver during church activities. Moms and dads are often unable to use their gifts to serve their church because caregiving consumes all of their time. If they were not attending children's Sunday school with their child, or taking turns babysitting at home on Sunday mornings, what would they want to be doing instead? This question is worth asking. You might discover an amazing choir member, hospitality specialist, or Old Testament scholar. You might also discover a person longing to grow spiritually in a community of believers without an opportunity to do so.

The very last question is one of the most important: "Who else would benefit from this conversation?" Special needs families do not always advertise their needs, diagnosis, hurt, or fears to the larger community. Very often, however, they network with families who are experiencing similar circumstances. You may know of only one family affected by special needs in your congregation when you start this process of asking, but chances are high you will discover other families by word of mouth as you begin asking questions.

This networking connection also provides a valuable bridge for outreach to the community. Michelle participates in a group of thirty moms who all have children with autism. She is the only mom of the group that attends church. In sharing how her church embraces her family, she has been able to invite families to visit and experience the love of God through an inclusive body of believers.

Please remember that disability affects people from all seasons and walks of life. Spouses of a person with a disability, children of adult members with disabilities, or the individual who lives with chronic illness, hearing loss, dementia, physical limitations, etc. should also be asked for their story and needs. The questions and answers might be different, but the need for a place to worship, fellowship, serve, and grow is the same for every individual.

A Side Note

If you have come to the conclusion that you do not even have one family in your church congregation to approach with this conversation, do not despair. Ask your congregation whom they would like to invite to VBS, youth group, church, etc. but have not because special needs are involved. Often your church community is connected to several families with special needs that they just have not felt comfortable inviting to church. In addition, reach out to your local school district, therapy centers, or nonprofit associations. Ask what you can do to support their efforts and the families they serve. By seeking out the special needs community, a bridge to your church family will be built on solid ground.

Step 2: Listen

Having in-depth, targeted conversations with special needs families often stirs up a symphony of emotions and dreams. Perhaps you are also affected by special needs and personally understand the struggles and the triumphs outlined in your interviews. Either way, you are angered by hurts sustained and gratified by blessings received. It can make you decide that you will immediately move heaven and earth to make sure each family member is completely cared for and embraced. It can make you say with confidence, "We will have a monthly respite program, a buddy ministry, a sensory suite, a support group for moms, and train the whole church in disability awareness in six months."

Many churches are stuck here, wanting to do everything but not knowing how to do anything. Often, really listening is the key. Did you come into the conversation expecting every family to beg for respite, but what they really desired is for their teen to be included in youth group? Perhaps you started this process dreaming of a specially outfitted sensory room, but parents continue to share their desire for full inclusion. Whatever the scenario, be willing to put your dream aside for the moment, and tally up the needs that have been expressed.

A Word on Leadership

Listening to Leadership

Listening to your church leadership's experiences and feelings is just as important as listening to families and individuals. Some may have had negative experiences with previous attempts of others to do special needs ministry. Some may have had no experience at all and have considerable questions to answer before the ministry can move forward. Regardless, you will never understand the road map of establishing effective disability ministry in your church without listening to your leadership.

You may discover that your church leaders believe that no change is necessary because they believe that all people are already fully welcome in their church. This is an opportunity to share, with permission, what you have learned through asking families about their experiences. There is nothing quite as effective as a true, personal story to help others understand what is needed.

Another important topic of conversation with leadership is to discuss which resources are available moving forward. What space is available if needed? Is there a budget or the opportunity to create a budget in the future? Is there opportunity to purchase curriculum if needed? People are ultimately the best resources, so discussing your church's process of utilizing volunteers is a good idea.

Be Prepared

Meeting with church leadership to express a need about which you are passionate is often the quickest way to become responsible for meeting that need. Be prepared to be the point person for this new endeavor if you suggest it. In addition, be prepared for an enthusiastic blessing from your church leadership to move forward without any next steps offered during that conversation. The next step in this sequence of five will continue to move things in the right direction with or without direction from your leaders once you have their blessing.

Step 3: Plan

You have asked the right questions of individuals, families, and leadership; you have listened to the answers. You have tallied up the needs and the resources available. It is time to begin planning and organizing the implementation of a fruitful ministry. This step often looks different from church to church. Your team size, organization, and responsibilities will depend on church size, culture, denominational influence, and existing ministry emphasis and programs.

Start Small

Starting small is starting smart, building a foundation that lasts even through leadership changes. Rather than implementing everyone's ideas at once under the heading of special needs ministry, concentrate your efforts on one idea at a time. Choose one need and see that need met from beginning to end. If that need requires ongoing ministry, make sure that ministry is fully established before beginning a new effort. Besides not asking and listening, starting too big is the most common mistake that makes a church's special needs ministry fold.

A Word of Caution

In most people's minds planning usually equates to creating a program. Programs are designed to bring results, like a weight loss program or a beginning arts program. Ministry, on the other hand, is an avenue to meet the needs of people. People and their needs change and grow, while programs typically do not. Remember that fruitful ministry is about all people having access to the gospel and a place to grow in grace, fellowship, worship, and service. If this can be accomplished without starting another church program, then a new church program is not needed. So, as you proceed, continue to focus on people, not on programs.

Meeting Immediate Needs

When starting, deal first with the immediate, practical needs that do not require a new ministry plan, just thoughtful, creative application of resources. Are there pressing needs that can be handled through an existing ministry or servants in the church?

Perhaps a medical emergency has created a financial burden for a family affected by special needs that can be alleviated through a benevolence fund. Maybe the greatest need is a reliable adult who can drive siblings to youth group so mom can take a younger child to therapy each week. I once had a women's Bible study approach me to ask if I knew of anyone's house that needed to be cleaned on a regular basis—they felt that housekeeping was one of their gifts. Earlier that month a couple had shared with me their frustration at not being able to keep a clean house because of the husband's work schedule and the wife's significant physical disability. Once connected, the Bible study and the couple both felt loved and part of the body of Christ. While none of these examples fall under the traditional heading of disability ministry, each demonstrates the love of Christ and helps provide the support all families need to be fully functioning members of the kingdom.

Some churches are great at meeting immediate needs and helping families and individuals get through times of crisis. They share the best casseroles, send emergency babysitters in the middle of the night, and plaster hospital rooms with homemade cards and flowers. Know that families affected by special needs often have more than their seemingly fair share of emergencies and will need those casseroles, cards, and extra helping hands each time, maybe for years to come.

Do not confuse this needed short-term outpouring of love with effective long-term disability ministry. The heart of your church's special needs ministry will be based on the individual dreams and desires expressed over time.

Long-Term Planning

Whether the ministry is serving and including children, teens, young adults, or adults, start with the people that God has already brought to your church and their day-to-day involvement. You will hear over and over again how parents and kids of all ages desire access to the existing programs and people in your church. While full inclusion is not always feasible or desirable, a degree of inclusion is almost always possible and beneficial. Supported inclusion, providing one-on-one interaction within the group setting, seems to be the most common and reasonable answer to how to make church and its people accessible.

The key to finding the right balance is never losing sight of the eternal purpose: How will this person and this person's family best meet Jesus, grow in grace, and serve with their God-given gifts while fully participating in the body of Christ? Filter all your questions and decisions through this perspective and it will be very hard to do the wrong thing.

Plan for Maturity

We often encounter youth and adults who wistfully describe how they were integrated into their church's children's ministry, but active planning for their involvement dwindled as they grew older. As you create plans to include individuals based on their expressed needs, understand that their needs will change. As they age, some individuals will have increased needs for accessibility and acceptance, and some will have less. Most people with disabilities do not grow out of their special needs, and we should plan accordingly from the beginning.

Ministry Models

There are many models of ministry that have been effectively used to meet the needs of church congregations and communities. Use these ideas, along with the direction from your church leadership, as a starting place to explore the best way of meeting the needs families and individuals within your church express. Here are just a few examples that should help your own ideas take shape. For more detailed information on these models and other related topics, check out the other resources made available by Joni and Friends.

- **Buddy Ministry** – an adult, teenager, or peer is paired with an individual who has special needs during the typical activities of church life. Churches often call these individuals by a name that identifies the relationship between them and the special needs children they are supporting. Some examples of names include Sidekicks, Friends, and Heroes. These buddies support those with special needs so that they can participate to their full potential. The buddies are not babysitters. The buddies do make sure their partners are being evangelized and discipled with opportunities to serve, worship, and fellowship.
  - Parents and siblings should not be buddies with their family member as this can limit the Christian relationships a person with a disability can have and does not provide the family members with their own appropriate relationships.
  - Buddies can be useful in the following:

- Children's Sunday school
- Awana or other programs
- Vacation Bible school
- Youth group
- Adult Sunday school
- Worship service
- Children's church
- Church-wide functions like potlucks, service projects, and fellowship nights
- Mission trips
- Retreats and camps

- **Sensory Space** – an environment where individuals who need a break from typical sensory input (like worship music or people talking) or who need sensory input not found in a typical church environment (like the feeling of motion or being wrapped tightly in a blanket) can have their sensory needs met so that they can continue to be evangelized and discipled.
  - Sensory spaces come in all shapes and sizes:
    - A bag that a person can pull sensory items from as needed in his or her typical environment
    - A corner of a classroom that can hold a tent or squishy chair

- A separate room specially outfitted with non-fluorescent lights and sensory soothing materials and furniture

- **Self-Contained Instruction** – an environment where individuals who do not learn well in, or do not benefit from, the typical environments with their peers can be discipled effectively. This environment can be highly successful if supported inclusion is not effective.
  - Self-contained instruction can:
    - Be utilized during a portion of time at church, mixed with supported inclusion
    - Be tailored through typical curriculum to meet the intellectual needs of participants
    - Benefit from reverse inclusion, where small groups of peers enter the self-contained environment for meaningful relationships

- **Respite** – an opportunity for caregivers to have a break from caregiving while allowing the person who is cared for an opportunity to have fun with friends in a safe environment. Respite can have a spiritual emphasis, or it can simply be a time of sharing Christ's love through relationship.
  - Respite is often offered in the following ways:

- Quarterly or monthly
- As a night out for parents
- As a morning out for caregivers
- During support groups for parents and siblings
- With a theme or a party

- **Support Groups** – a time for moms, dads, couples, siblings, or people with disabilities to gather for encouragement and support from others sharing their experience. This should not replace the larger community of the church body but can be a transformative addition to it.
  - Support groups are most successful:
    - With a facilitator who is emotionally healthy and biblically sound
    - When they meet often and stay on a regular schedule
    - When parameters are set for sharing unsolicited advice
    - When they are truly confidential

It Takes a Team

Whatever ministry models you decide to implement will benefit greatly from a team. By starting with a team from the very beginning, you reduce the risk of burnout and the risk of everything falling apart if something should happen to the leader.

Again, every church culture, structure, and size will dictate the most sensible organization of a team, but for reference a comprehensive team could consist of the following positions:

- **Ministry Coordinator** – This is the point person with administrative gifts and positive relationships with church leadership and families, and who is willing to be the responsible go-to person.
- **Family Liaison** – This is the person who meets with each family/individual to complete the Family Ministry Profile, and who will stay aware of and communicate any changes necessary in the ensuing plan.
- **Volunteer Coordinator** – This person recruits volunteers, places them in the right service positions, and makes sure they are trained.
- **Curriculum Coordinator** – This person modifies existing curriculum or provides new curriculum for individuals with intellectual disabilities, those needing physical accommodations, etc. Examples of modifications

include providing large-print materials for the visually impaired, sensory items that help communicate Bible truths, or craft items that are easy to use for a person with low muscle tone.

- **Leadership Liaison** – This is the person with full access to church staff and leadership that can be a positive bridge of open communication.
- **Family Consultant(s)** – This person should be related to the individual affected by special needs, like the parent of a child with special needs, who is willing to be a sounding board as needed.
- **Ministry Consultant(s)** – This individual should be a special needs teacher, therapist, etc. Rather than doing the week-to-week management of the ministry, this person can share expertise as needed to train volunteers, troubleshoot a difficult behavioral situation, etc.
- **Prayer Coordinator** – This person coordinates ongoing, specific prayer for the leadership, participants, and fruitfulness of your ministry.
- **Existing Staff Members** – Individuals leading existing ministries in the church can be active allies or enemies depending on how they are approached and included in this process. If your ministry endeavors involve an existing

program that has a leader, please include this person from the beginning to promote unity and protect from misunderstandings. Pull in leadership that will shepherd individuals with special needs as they age so that their transition into other programs is successful.

- **Volunteers** – These individuals are the heart of any ministry. Consider partnering with existing church programs like the youth group, college ministry, and men's and women's Bible studies for mutually beneficial opportunities. Volunteers should be well screened, background checked, and trained.

Sharing the Load

In some situations, one person takes on all of these responsibilities at the beginning. Other churches have two or three who share the load. Carefully consider the "legacy" plan of your ministry. If the ministry leader were unable to continue, do enough people have access to and investment in the ministry that individuals with special needs would continue to belong in your church?

Having a leadership liaison helps ensure one person is not shouldering the full responsibility for the entire special needs ministry. Having an appointed person in leadership circles to filter all ministry events and programs and to emphasize how families and individuals with special needs can be involved is very helpful. For example, the children's pastor of a large church requested automatic accessible doors at the main entrance of a new building plan. After initial hesitancy and much conversation, the building committee voted to include the accessible doors. Because this pastor was already involved in the planning and was a member of the leadership group, this church is moving forward with accessibility, without the need for the special needs ministry coordinator to become involved.

A Word to Small Churches

If you represent a small church, it may seem that your available resources are too limited to launch and maintain a specials needs ministry. In reality, small churches are often so integrated among leaders, programs, and ministry endeavors that needs are met and people are embraced naturally and simply. Including a student with special needs in a small church's children or youth ministry is often easier than in a large church because programs are more flexible. Teacher-to-student ratios can be small enough to allow personalized instruction without the need for extra volunteers. Do not let the extensive list of volunteer positions scare you; many small churches naturally meet the needs of those with disabilities and may only have a special needs ministry coordinator to keep tabs on families and needs as they arise.

A Word to Large Churches

Large churches typically have the manpower, existing programs, space, and other resources to launch a sustainable special needs ministry fairly easily. The delicate part is making sure you go through the established channels of communication and honor existing policies and procedures. Talking with each staff member or ministry leader that new ministry endeavors will impact helps keep everyone unified and can remove roadblocks along the way. Working closely with a leadership partner is necessary in any size church, but this is especially important in a large church to help navigate existing structures. In the midst of this navigation it can be challenging to keep the focus on people rather than the program.

A Word on Special Needs Professionals as Ministry Leaders

One of the most common reasons churches give for not pursuing disability ministry is that they do not have a special education expert willing to take the reins. Expecting the special needs professionals in your congregation to take on full responsibility for something they already do full-time is often unrealistic due to time restraints and the need for a break. In reality, having a leader gifted in administration that loves people is much more effective. Experts and resources can fill in the information gaps of running a special needs ministry, but nothing can replace the value of having an organized, invested leader.

A Word on Parents as Ministry Leaders

Parents of children with special needs or other caregivers often assume the role of ministry coordinator. God has used the talents, experiences, and passion of parents who have children with special needs around the globe to shape the church into a fully inclusive body. We are grateful for the many parents who have answered God's calling on their lives to become ministry leaders.

While this is a true calling from God for many parents to use their gifts in the church, other parents assume this role for reasons that are not ideal:

- The parents approach church leadership with their desire for their child to be fully discipled through a special needs ministry. The parents are told that since they have the idea for the ministry, it must mean God has equipped them and called them to run the ministry.

- Parents request accommodations for their child to be included. Leadership is not opposed to the accommodations but requires the parents to provide the person or materials since they are the "experts."

- Some parents have a strong desire to control each environment and opportunity that touches their child with special needs. They may not trust others to lead a ministry that impacts their family, because of past experiences or other factors.

Consider each of these ways parents may become leaders in special needs ministry through the lens of the following analogy. Imagine a world-renowned cardiologist having a massive heart attack. He knows immediately to call for help because of his expertise in the field.

Imagine if the first responders said, "You really knew exactly when to call for help! That just confirms how gifted of a cardiologist you are. We are convinced that with your knowledge and experience you are best suited to treat yourself. We fully support you." This is like telling parents who are asking for help that they must have been called to run the ministry because they brought up the need.

An equally unhelpful response from first responders to the cardiologist would be, "Since you are the expert, you probably have the best medicine and procedures, so we will not provide anything for you. We wish you the very best on your recovery!" Expecting parents to provide accommodations without any collaboration and help from the church community is very much like this response.

Finally, imagine if the cardiologist drove himself to the hospital and refused the help of nurses and doctors, saying instead that he had the most experience and knew what was best. His recovery would hardly be notable for its success. Some parents place themselves in this situation out of fear and the desire for control.

The illustration of a heart attack is appropriate because families affected by special needs are often in personal times of crisis, whether it is a lack of fellowship, spiritual encouragement, or opportunity to serve in their areas of giftedness, or because of marital or other family stress. Caregiving is time-consuming and does not often leave room for other endeavors.

If you are a parent of a child with special needs and you feel called to lead a disability ministry, please carefully consider your available time, energy, and passion. A healthy leader is much more likely to foster a healthy ministry than a leader who is constantly stretched too thin and whose first priorities lie elsewhere. You may be spiritually and emotionally healthy now, but carefully consider if you will be able to maintain that health while running a ministry.

If you are a pastor or a member of church leadership, please carefully consider what you ask of parents and caregivers. They need the opportunity to worship, fellowship, serve, and grow in grace as much as the person for whom they give care. Healthy caregivers foster healthy families, which foster healthy churches. A parent of a child with special needs is not automatically capable of or qualified for running a special needs ministry. Consider reviewing the steps of asking and listening before deciding who should fill ministry leadership roles.

Job Descriptions

When asking people to volunteer, to coordinate, or to fill any position of service, it is helpful to have concrete job descriptions. These can grow and change over time, but having a basic outline of what a person's responsibilities, skill requirements, and terms of service are sets everyone up for success.

As you pull together a team and build these job descriptions, stress that no experience is required to serve. Interviewing families, finding out volunteers' spiritual gifts and passions, or planning a themed respite event does not require a person with specialized experience. Instead, focus on the needs at hand and those whom God has gifted to meet them.

Step 4: Train

Because you have asked families, individuals, and leadership what the true needs and resources are, because you have listened to the answers, and you have pulled together a team and a plan, you are ready to train. Training is the glue that holds the pieces of the ministry together. There are typically three groups of people that require comprehensive training for a church community to become inclusive: the special needs ministry team, church leadership, and the congregation.

Comprehensive Training

Training takes on fresh life when done by multiple people and through multiple experiences. Inviting medical and educational professionals, family members, disability ministry experts, experienced volunteers, other ministry leaders, and people with disabilities to train will give a comprehensive overview of disability ministry.

Train Your Team
Training your leadership team and hands-on volunteers is essential to a healthy ministry. Training can

take a variety of forms and is never completed. Conditioning your team to learn from mistakes, to take an active interest in disability awareness, and to continually learn from the people they are serving help retain active members of your team.

There are several training topics that should be addressed with any special needs ministry team before disability ministry is formally launched. You will know best what information gaps need to be filled for your unique team and what training has already happened through your church's standard volunteer procedures.

Here is a list of training topics that are helpful to cover with a special needs ministry team:

- Disability Awareness and Etiquette
  - What language to use and not use regarding people affected by disability
  - How to interact with people's mobility equipment like wheelchairs
  - Basics of disabilities that are present in your church and common in your community

- Job Descriptions and Ministry Procedures
  - The five Ws of ministry

- Why do we do special needs ministry?
- Who is my supervisor? With whom do I interact to complete my responsibility?
- What is my responsibility? What procedures are in place that I need to follow?
- When do I serve and for how long?
- Where does this service take place? Where are the materials and information stored that I will need to access?

- The Ministry Plan
  - A synopsis of the comprehensive ministry plan assures people that their role is valuable in accomplishing the goal.
  - A Day in the Life – This approach walks a person through a period of service step-by-step, moment by moment, from the very beginning to the very end. It is a very effective training tool for new volunteers who are nervous about how to serve effectively.

Training opportunities can be scheduled in a variety of ways. Some churches host mandatory group trainings once or twice a year that involve all volunteers and leaders. Other churches have orientation trainings sprinkled throughout the year for new volunteers who join the team. Some churches train new volunteers by pairing them as a shadow with an experienced volunteer. Be creative and proactive in your training, and people will be grateful for the insight.

Train Church Leadership

If you have made it this far, you have the blessing of your church leadership to pursue disability ministry. Many ministry leaders have expressed discomfort in talking with and referring to people with disabilities because of their lack of experience and training. They may have provided the go-ahead to start the ministry but still do not know how to effectively engage the very individuals the ministry aims to reach.

Instead of asking leaders to attend another meeting or training, ask if you can get on the agenda at a staff meeting or whatever venue your church uses to get the leadership together. Use that time to share a personal story of how the special needs ministry is meeting needs, and share what needs still exist. Teach basics of disability awareness. Ask for questions and feedback, and answer them graciously. You will find that training church leadership is really about providing disability awareness and etiquette training.

Good church leadership thinks about how to protect and provide for the entire church congregation. Because these leaders have the needs of the whole body in mind, they will ask if special insurance is needed, what liability is involved, who is taking responsibility, etc. Fully answering these questions may seem disheartening when you are trying to discuss acceptance and accessibility, but it is a necessary step—essential to aligning your leadership team behind the cause of including people with disabilities. For the record, at the time this book is being written, no special insurance is required, and there is no additional liability assumed because a person has special needs, unless medical care is provided. If medical care is necessary for a person's involvement, those individuals often have a nurse or personal care assistant (PCA) that can attend activities with them.

Allowing church leadership to "experience" disability for a short length of time is a very effective way to provide instant awareness for a particular disability. Treat a church leader to lunch on the condition that the leader uses a wheelchair for the entire outing.

Provide a communication board to be used for ten minutes during the next staff meeting. Smear Vaseline on glasses to be worn during a Wednesday night activity to simulate vision impairment. Be creative and positive in sharing disability awareness.

Finally, invite your church leadership to interact with people who have special needs. Whether it is hosting a small dinner party in your home, asking your pastor to give a devotional during a respite event, or bringing a friend with special needs by the church office, nothing can replace relationship as a tool for teaching disability awareness.

Train the Congregation

Whether your special needs ministry takes shape in existing programs and structures of the church or is launched as a totally new endeavor, cultivating an attitude of inclusion and acceptance in your church congregation is imperative. Visibility of special needs ministry opportunities is vital for the health of the ministry. By having multiple touch points with the congregation, you effectively recruit new volunteers, maintain leadership support, and boldly proclaim that your church body embraces people affected by disability.

Families frequently leave churches with established special needs ministries and church leadership that have expressed their support of including loved ones with special needs. They leave reluctantly, not because of the lack of ministry, or because of the leadership, but because the general attitude and actions of the congregation convey that their family is not welcome. As one father of a son with special needs once told me, "We found lots of churches that would tolerate us, but not accept us."

Members of the congregation may not realize the impact of their comments, facial expressions, and actions. Many times people with no special needs experience are so fearful of saying or doing the wrong thing that they do not say or do anything at all, leaving the family with special needs feeling isolated and excluded. Without training in disability awareness and etiquette, the congregation will not know what is and is not appropriate and loving.

For example, take a young man with autism who enjoys participating in worship services but finds shaking hands and looking others in the eye during the greeting time to be physically painful. Without awareness and etiquette training, a church member may assume the young man is being rude by refusing to shake his hand and meet his eye. This member may reprimand the young man and his parents for his "poor" behavior. With general training on interacting with individuals with autism or people who have a hidden disability, this church member will have a completely different response to choose.

Training the congregation is a never-ending process, but it can be done in very manageable and highly impactful ways. Examples include the following:

- Interviewing a family with special needs during church
- Creating short video testimonies that show what life is like on a daily basis for church members with special needs
- Training ushers, greeters, parking attendants, and those responsible for hospitality how to welcome and assist families affected by special needs
- Preaching about and to people affected by disability, as appropriate
- Publishing an awareness guide on your website
- Presenting short presentations to Sunday school classes, small groups, Bible studies, etc.

When thinking of who makes up a congregation, we often only think of adults. However, children and youth are vital pieces of the culture of the congregation and are often the ones who interact most with those affected by special needs. Consider how to train the classmates, small group friends, and event participants about their peers' special needs. Often children take people with special needs at face value and simply need to know how best to communicate with their friend.

Becoming Experts

Training may seem overwhelming at first, especially for people who are not disability experts. Rather than trying to become an expert in the broad field of special needs, focus on becoming an expert on the people affected by special needs in your congregation. Parents of children with special needs generally were not experts before the diagnosis arrived in their family, but they became experts on their child and how to interact with their child's diagnosis. The church body can do the same.

Step 5: Launch

All of the asking, listening, planning, and training you have done will be for nothing if you do not put what you have learned into action. Do not let fear prevent you from experiencing the blessing of including all people in the life of your church.

Common Fears

Churches get stuck on the launchpad as a result of several common fears:

- The need in the community is so large. What if everyone comes at once and totally overwhelms the ministry and church?
- Volunteers seem to come and go in our church community. What if we cannot provide something that we have promised and we hurt someone's feelings?
- We are receiving resistance from the leader of a certain program. What if they cause the ministry to fail?
- What if we do not have any families with disabilities engage in the ministry?

Notice that all of these fears revolve around what-if statements. Instead of focusing on what might happen, focus on the information you have at hand. You know the needs, you know how to meet them, and you have a plan and team in place. None of the what-ifs will be more disappointing to your families than going through all these steps and then not acting.

How to Launch

Pick a launch date and stick with it. Small trial runs before a public launch can also be helpful. Know that it will never be perfect, and there will always be surprises; this is the nature of all ministry endeavors, not just disability ministry!

To help put things in perspective, consider the difference between launching your ministry like a slingshot versus a hot-air balloon.

Launching Like a Slingshot

Slingshots are great for a thrilling, breathless moment of anticipating hitting a target. It does not take much skill to load a slingshot and fire it at the target. Unfortunately, instead of the bull's-eye, other things are often hit and broken in the process. Slingshots do not provide an opportunity to correct the course of the ammunition once it has left the sling. In other words, you have one shot.

Launching disability ministry like a slingshot very rarely produces a long-standing, fruitful ministry. Without the opportunity to correct the course as you go, the ministry endeavor might totally miss the mark. You might actually end up hurting others in the process. Collecting more resources to "load the slingshot" again may not be possible.

Launching Like a Hot-Air Balloon

Hot-air balloons are completely different from slingshots. It takes time, planning, and energy to get them in the air, but once up, the sky is the limit. The pilot of the hot-air balloon uses heat to control the height of the balloon, constantly seeking air currents at different altitudes. These currents then drive the balloon in the direction the pilot wishes to go.

Launching a disability ministry like a hot-air balloon allows the Holy Spirit to guide you. He is the wind that gives direction to your ministry. He has given you gifts, resources, and knowledge to use as the heat to readjust as needed. By launching in this quiet, thoughtful way, your resources will last and provide for a fruitful ministry.

The Blessings

Launching a fruitful disability ministry will bring unexpected blessings to your church body. Your church will become irresistible to those outside and those struggling inside when they see how you welcome, include, and disciple people with disabilities and their families.

You will also find that evangelizing and discipling those affected by disability helps produce stronger disciples of your typical church members. Members who have not found a passionate place of service often excel at serving in disability ministry and seem to find their ministry "home." Because disability ministry can take place across all programs and initiatives, it brings the church together and helps prevent programs and traditions from becoming more important than people.

Ultimately, effective disability ministry shouts to a world that values perfection, superficial beauty, and power that God and his people value those who seem weak, who depend on others, and who appear insignificant. Disability ministry proclaims that the gospel is for all people who have faith in Jesus, regardless of their abilities, social standing, or culture. There is no clearer picture of the good news of Jesus Christ than Christians living out 1 Corinthians 12:22–26:

> The parts of the body that seem to be weaker are indispensable, and on those parts of the body that we think less honorable we bestow the greater honor . . . God has so composed the body, giving greater honor to the part that lacked it, that there may be no division in the body, but that members may have the same care for one another. If one member suffers, all suffer together; if one member is honored, all rejoice together.

If a church cares for and honors those who seem to be weaker, the end result is that all members rejoice together. May you and your church experience the joy of disability ministry!

The *Irresistible* Church

Luke 14 commands Christ followers to "Go quickly . . . find the blind, the lame, and the crippled . . . and compel them to come in!" While this sounds inspiring and daunting, exciting and overwhelming, motivating and frightening, all at the same time, what does it actually mean? How do we live and function within the church in such a way that families affected by disability are compelled to walk through our doors to experience the body of Christ?

We can certainly *compel* them by offering programs, ministries, events, and other church activities, but what if the compelling aspect was more about heart, culture, acceptance and embracing? What if our churches were overflowing with the hope of Jesus Christ . . . a hope not simply for those who look the part or "fit in," but rather a hope to all, including the marginalized, the downtrodden and outcast?

Becoming *irresistible* is more than programs and activities—it is about a transformational work in our hearts . . . first as individuals and then as the body of Christ. *Irresistible* allows us to see each individual as he or she truly is: created in the image of God (Genesis 1:26-27), designed purposely as a masterpiece (Psalm 139:13-14), instilled with purpose, plans and dreams (Jeremiah 29:11), and a truly indispensable member of the kingdom of God (1 Corinthians 12:22).

Irresistible is a mindset, a perspective, an awareness. It is the ability to see the world through the eyes of Christ and love people where they are, knowing that God has designed an amazing future and hope for every person on this earth. *Irresistible* captures the heart of the church as it should be—how else do we explain the rapid growth and intense attraction to the church in the book of Acts? People were lining up to join this movement of people in spite of the intense persecution and ridicule. The heart of God was embodied through the people of God by the Spirit of God . . . and that is simply *irresistible*!

The Irresistible Church Series is designed to help not only shape and transform the heart of the Church, but also to provide the practical steps and activities to put *flesh* around the *heart* of the Church. Thank you for responding to the call to become *irresistible* - it will not happen overnight, but it will happen. As with all good things, it requires patience and perseverance, determination and dedication, and ultimately an underlying trust in the faithfulness of God. May God bless you on this journey and be assured that you are not alone—there are many on the path of *irresistible*.

For more information or to join the community, please visit www.irresistiblechurch.org.

and Friends
INTERNATIONAL DISABILITY CENTER

Joni and Friends was established in 1979 by Joni Eareckson Tada, who at 17 was injured in a diving accident, leaving her a quadriplegic. Since its inception, Joni and Friends has been dedicated to extending the love and message of Christ to people who are affected by disability whether it is the disabled person, a family member, or friend. Our objective is to meet the physical, emotional, and spiritual needs of this group of people in practical ways.

Joni and Friends is committed to recruiting, training, and motivating new generations of people with disabilities to become leaders in their churches and communities. Today, the Joni and Friends International Disability Center serves as the administrative hub for an array of programs which provide outreach to thousands of families affected by disability around the globe. These include two radio programs, an award-winning television series, the Wheels for the World international wheelchair distribution ministry, Family Retreats which provide respite for those with disabilities and their families, Field Services to provide church training along with educational and inspirational resources at a local level, and the Christian Institute on Disability to establish a firm biblical worldview on disability-related issues.

From local neighborhoods to the far reaches of the world, Joni and Friends is striving to demonstrate to people affected by disability, in tangible ways, that God has not abandoned them—he is with them—providing love, hope, and eternal salvation.

Coming Soon in the Irresistible Church Series

Engaging Game Changers
Recruiting and Coaching Volunteers for Disability Ministry

The breadth of impact any ministry has for the individuals they serve is dependent on the volunteers who are recruited to be the hands and feet of Jesus. This resource will train you as a ministry leader to identify and recruit, thoroughly train, then release volunteers who will serve families affected by special needs effectively and with the love of Christ.

To receive first notice of upcoming resources, including respite, inclusive worship and support groups, please contact us at churchrelations@joniandfriends.org.

Coming Soon in the Irresistible Church Series

We've Got This!
Providing Respite for Families Affected by Disability

Parents who have children with disabilities are often isolated, exhausted, and grieving. Respite events can woo these parents over the threshold of the church by satisfying an urgent need. This manual is a practical guide that provides every tool you need for planning a successful respite event.

To receive first notice of upcoming resources, including respite, inclusive worship and support groups, please contact us at churchrelations@joniandfriends.org.

Other Recommended Resources

Beyond Suffering®
Classic Edition

Beyond Suffering: A Christian View on Disability Ministry provides you with a roadmap to an effective and inspiring disability ministry. *Beyond Suffering* is a comprehensive course that gives an overview of the theological and practical underpinnings of the movement. It will equip you to think critically, compassionately and clearly about the complex issues that impact people with disabilities and their families and to confidently bring them the love of Christ.

ISBN: 978-0-9838484-0-0
272 pages · 8.5" x 11"
Includes CD-ROM

Beyond Suffering®
Student Edition

Beyond Suffering for the Next Generation: A Christian View on Disability Ministry will equip young people to consider the issues that affect people with disabilities and their families, and inspire them to action. Students who embrace this study will gain confidence to join a growing, worldwide movement that God is orchestrating to fulfill Luke 14:21-23: "Go out quickly into the streets and alleys of the town and bring in the poor, the crippled, the blind, and the lame.... so that my house will be full."

ISBN: 978-0-9838484-6-2
304 pages · 8.5" x 11"
Includes CD-ROM

Special Needs
Smart Pages

If you want to help children with special needs know Jesus and have a vital relationship with God, you need the Special Needs Smart Pages. This essential, comprehensive resource will help you reach out to kids with a variety of special needs. Learn how to meet the physical, social, emotional and spiritual needs of disabled children, how to recruit and train leaders and teachers for a special needs ministry and how to help kids with special needs discover and use their unique gifts to serve God!

ISBN: 978-0-8307-4719-1
328 pages · 8.5" x 11"
Includes DVD & CD-ROM

www.joniandfriends.org · P.O. Box 3333, Agoura Hills, CA 91376
(818) 707-5664 · Fax: (818) 707-2391 TTY: (818) 707-9707

Customizable Resources from the Book

Available for Download at
http://www.joniandfriends.org/church-relations/

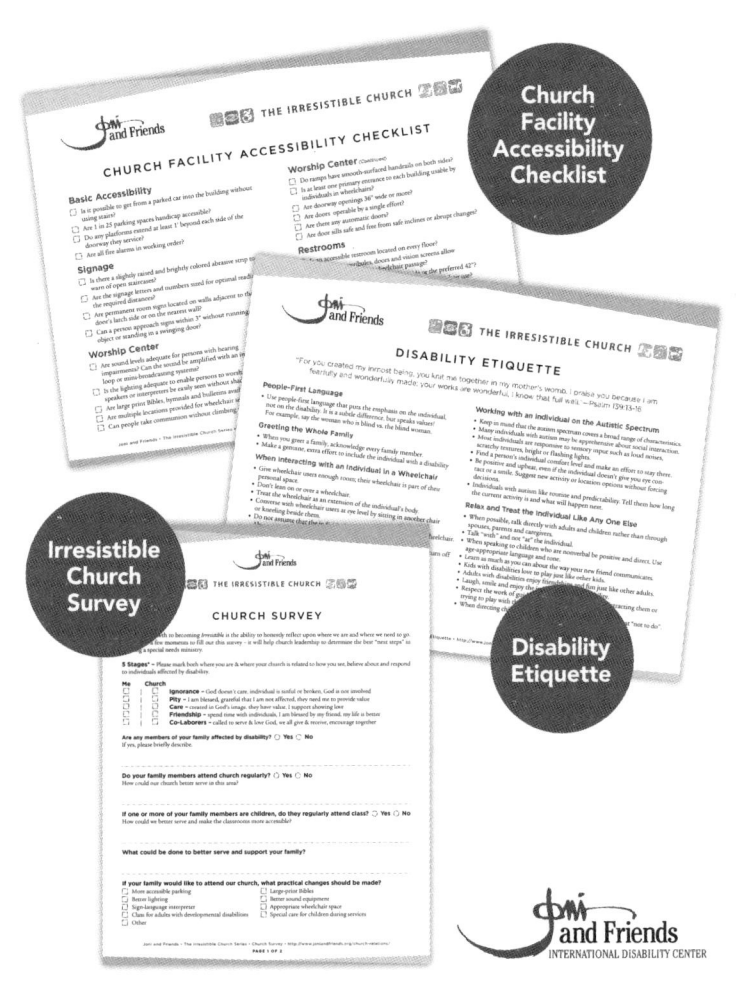

Church Facility Accessibility Checklist

Irresistible Church Survey

Disability Etiquette